This book  memory of my grandmother Mrs. Lucy R. Ledbetter - Lewis, A mighty powerful women gone to be in Heaven with the LORD. She instilled in me to be faithful to CHRIST, be honest and be a strong independent woman.

I also dedicate this book to my grandmother Mrs. Allonia Lewis - Pruitt, A women who has always made me aware that the LORD should be placed first in my life and that HE is always there when I need HIM. She is indeed a survivor!

Also, to the memory of one of my best friends (sister) Tamika James. Look sis, I finally did it!

CHAPTERS

Introduction

Do You Remember?

Prayed Up

Still I Smile

The Teacher

How can any GOOD come out of me?!?

Yet Holding On

Look At Me Now

Valuable Information

Statistics

Hotline Numbers

Exit

St. John 3:16 KJV reads: For GOD so loved the world that he gave his only begotten Son, that whosoever believeth in him should not perish, but have everlasting life.

Introduction

Phil. 4:13 KJV reads, I can do all things through Christ which strengthens me. This is a scripture true to my own heart and I believe that it should be the anthem for all women who have endured a great deal of discomfort, agony and/or pain from a man. This book will introduce you to several women that I am very familiar with and close to. They have each endured some form of violence, tragedy, and/or heartaches & pains. But through it all they continued to stand on the promises of GOD and say to him "Here I Am – LORD I Surrender."

They have each personally encouraged me, in some way or the other to continue to strive forward and I pray that you too; will be encouraged upon reading each of their personal testimonies given to me to share with you.

According to the bible when a man marries his wife, he is to forsake all others and cling to his wife and become one. We hear this repeatedly, yet these women have all experience some form of neglect, abuse, and/or betrayal from a man. What happened did he not know this? Was he never made aware of this? Or did he just not care? Follow along with me and we shall see exactly what these women experienced and how they continue to tell the LORD "Here I Am – LORD I Surrender."

Do You Remember?
(Author: Tawana D. Pruitt)

You said that you loved me
Do You Remember?

You promised to never hurt me
Do You Remember?

I was always crying and sad
Do You Remember?

How I was never glad
Do You Remember?

You tore me down to feel bad
Do You Remember?

The moment I found myself
Do You Remember?

Oh how I remember!
The look of surprise on your face
Do You Remember?

As I took my rightful place
Do You Remember?

Prayed Up

Proverbs 3:5 - 6 KJV reads, Trust in the LORD with all of your heart. Lean not to your own understanding and always acknowledge HIM; HE will direct your path. Having faith that the LORD will provide, being from a little city in Mississippi, born to uneducated parents that stressed to me the importance of an education. I was raised on a farm and was told that working hard, getting a good education and being a good Christian that I could have a good life and be successful.

I finished high school in 1960 and immediately following that I made what I consider to be a fatal mistake. I got pregnant and married a man that made my life a living hell for eighteen and a half years. This man tried to kill me by shooting me in the lower part of my abdomen. He continued to try to discharge his weapon at me. My mother stepped in the path while he was doing this. But GOD caused the gun to jam and not fire. Otherwise I and my mother both might have been killed at the hands of my husband. I thank HIM for protecting us both during that situation. I continue to carry a souvenir in my body to this day; my reminder of what I went through with my husband; "A Bullet."

There were many physical beatings following this incident; as well as, constant verbal abuse. Because the physical abuse that I encounter I suffer from a regular reminder known as epileptic seizures.

Through all this heartache & pain I bore four children to my husband. My children were mentally scared from being witnesses to his violent outburst towards me. During all this my father-in-law resided with us and was just as mean spirited toward my children; as my husband was to each of us.

Despite all this turmoil I was able to hold a job for over eighteen years with a very reputable company. So that when I finally found the strength and the courage to divorce my abuser, I was able to sustain, maintain and provide for not only me, but for my four children. There were many hardships that we went through, while living on the west side of Chicago. I was a single parent raising four children, working two jobs to make ends meet. Yet my faith in GOD sustained me.

In the mid-eighties I met and entered a relationship with yet another abusive man. This relationship was a very stormy off again, on again type of relationship. My faith has always been my rock. The relationship finally came to an end in 2008. During this relationship, my health began to fail; I suffered from a heart attack. But through it all I was able to draw upon my faith and know that the LORD would provide for me.

Today I currently live what I call the best part of my life. I have modeled for Turner Style, done photos for Essence Magazine and all these blessings at the age of 68. I do know that the LORD will provide. I praise HIM now, just as I did then. HE is my provider, my doctor when I am sick, and the shoulder that I cry upon when others fail to hear me. I thank HIM for loving me the way HE does.

.

Still I Smile
(Author: Tawana D. Pruitt)

When I look at myself in the mirror
Still I Smile…

As I grace others with my presence
Still I Smile…

While remembering my past as torrid as it may be
Still I Smile…

Thinking of the things that I've been through
Still I smile…

Laughing at the thought of you
Still I Smile…

Knowing that you regret this loss
Still I Smile…

No matter the COST!
Still I smile…

The Teacher

Psalms 90:1 KJV reads, Lord thou has been our dwelling place in all generations. I am the eldest of four siblings and the oldest grandchild on both sides, father and mother side of the family. I was also the first grandchild to finish high school and attend and graduate from college. I was born in the State of Mississippi where we were taught that if GOD takes you to it, that HE will carry you through it. That is what I have lived by since I was a little girl.

I was molested by a stepfather at the age of fourteen. I was very close to this man and it hurts me to this day when I think about what he did to me. And, how it led to me seeking the wrong attention from a man.

While seeking the wrong attention from men, I got pregnant at the age of sixteen by a married man and when I told him about my pregnancy he disappeared. He returned thirty years later, on my daughter's doorstep. When he showed up, she called me surprised. This was a day that neither of us thought would happen. She told me that he explained to her why he left. He told her "my mother threatened to have him locked up because he was having sex with an underage girl, and that she made him leave." My daughter believes him, and I think that there is some truth in this too. But he could've reached out to her, earlier on in her life. They communicate with one another to this day, because the relationship is of importance to my daughter.

I got married at the age of eighteen, and it was annulled two weeks later, due to physical abuse. I didn't give up on love after going through this marriage and the father of my child walking out on me.

I married my second husband at the age of twenty-five years old. He was a control freak, a Deacon in the church and was still in love with his first wife. When my daughter was twelve years old, he was charged with child molestation. He faced charges of fondling, finger penetration, and oral sex to a minor all of which were later dropped. But due to the embarrassment that he suffered we begin our journey of moving from state to state. It was almost like, what is he ashamed of? Did he do it? What is he covering up? Was It true?!?

He did treat my only child, a daughter different. He gave her everything that she ever asked for and wanted. He said that he never touched her, and I believed him; so, I stayed. We divorced after being married for thirteen or fourteen years, due to this.

I later lived with a man for five years, who was a whoremonger. He gambled and lied about everything that he could. He was charged and convicted of raping my daughter when she was 16 years old, while I was working a graveyard shift as a security officer. During all of this I lost custody of my daughter to my mother. My daughter married early and began having a family of her own, by a husband who beat her on a regular basis.

After my daughter moved away, I married my third husband, and this is when my life after Christ and backsliding began. He was very sorry and didn't believe in paying bills. He was verbally abusive always passing out threats to me. He preferred to hang out with children, ranging in ages from 13 - 18 years of age, who were his own children friends. The bible says that husband and wives are to cling to each other. I stopped going to church, but I still fasted and prayed. He had this saying "Who loves you baby?" My response was always God, my mother and my grandmother because I can depend on them and not on him.

I couldn't get along with his mother, because she liked to throw around the "N" word. Which, I found amusing, because my husband, her son was biracial, and she was also married to an African

American man. She told me that in order to love her grandchildren, I had to buy them things.

He stole my money out of the bank. I say it was my money, because I won it through a lawsuit against my job. I had finally had enough when my mother became ill. He told me to choose between him and my mother. I looked at him and said thank you and we later divorced. I moved in with my mother in order to take care of her and I continue to do just that to this date.

I am now happily married to a man that I met over the phone in 1998. We dated for ten years before we married. He only had one habit that I couldn't deal with that I knew of, and that was smoking marijuana. I said, Okay GOD you brought me a man, but he has a habit that I cannot deal with. So, I prayed and asked the LORD to remove the taste from his mouth, and he quit cold turkey. He is the best thing that has ever happened to me and I thank GOD for him every day.

He helped to care for my deceased grandmother and helps take care of my mother. He makes sure that I and my mother are both well taken care of. And he does all of this without complaining in the least way.

My relationship with GOD is awesome he has brought me through so much. I grew up in a one parent home, been raped, have had abusive relationship, have been shot at by another person. But through it all GOD was there, and I know this for a fact, and I thank HIM every day for HIS grace and mercy. I may have left the church, but I never stopped believing.

How can any GOOD come out of me?!?
(Author: Tawana D. Pruit)

I look into the mirror and I ask myself
How can any GOOD come out of me
I respond with a moan of disparity
For this man has driven it from me

LORD I ask thee every day
How can any GOOD come out of me
YOU respond with look into thy word
For your word is the driving force that guides me

I read, listen and I wait on you LORD
As I wonder; how can any GOOD come out of me
My prayers are being answered by thee
I see now the path I must take with thee

LORD please hear me as I cry and
I praise your name,
See these tears of gratitude as they
fall down my face
As I accept the gift that you have given
OH LORD I now can see the
GOOD that comes out of me.

Yet Holding On

Phil 3:14 KJV reads, I press toward the mark for the prize of the high calling of GOD in CHRIST JESUS.

I was born to a single mother at the age of 16, who struggled to finish high school and raise me. She finished high school, got married, re-married, re-married and finished college all while trying to raise me as a child. My mother was not a woman who expressed her feelings or the love that she had inside for me.

While being raised I suffered from child abuse, child molestation and rape. I was beaten if I didn't respond the way she thought that I should. I was beaten if I got in the way of her infidelities'. I was beaten if things failed to go the way she thought that they should.

I began to be molested at the young age of 4 or 5 by the hands of my mother's husband. He would come into my room on a regular basis and molest me. He fondled me, he penetrated my vagina with his fingers, and he "kissed" my vagina with his mouth as he described it. My mother provided him with all other opportunities in the world to molest me; because she was always asleep due to her anti-depressants and pain medications. She allowed this man to give me bathes at night and this was just another opportunity to be molested.

He was eventually charged with molestation, to include fondling, finger penetration and oral sex to a minor, he was arrested and went to trial. All I remember from that day is when we got to court, I was given medication that was said to be my prescribed antibiotics for a urinary tract infection caused by the molestation. I was drugged by mother with something that was not prescribed to me, because I began to show signs of sleepiness, dizziness and I had to be assisted to the witness stand. I was incoherent due to this medication, because while on the stand during the trial, my mind was saying yes but my mouth spoke the word no and I don't remember anything else. When I awaken at home, he was home sitting in the living room as a free man. Within weeks of his release, our home was up for sale and once it sold, we moved. We moved and moved and moved until I was in the 8th grade and my mother finally divorced him.

Experiencing child molestation for as long as I did, caused me to be withdrawn, standoffish, and antisocial. I didn't grow up with peers or friends as some may call them. I was ashamed and didn't want anyone to come over to play with me or spend time with me in the home. I only had my cousins and I was very protective over them. I didn't allow them to be alone with my abuser and I never let them out of my sight. As a child, that was a heavy burden, but I did what I felt I needed to do to protect them from him.

In school, I carried the behaviors of a defensive young girl. I would act out when and if a boy got too close to me. I even acted out when I was assigned a classroom with a male teacher. My grades would fluctuate, meaning I would carry all A's or all F's there was no in-between. The only thing I truly enjoyed while in school was chorus! It allowed me to sing and feel free in that moment.

I continue to have nightmares of these occurrences and at times it seems like it was just yesterday. He has since passed away. But before he died, he phoned me from the hospital to apologize and to tell me that he was wrong for violating me like that. I must say that I have just recently heard my mother admit that he molested me. After 30+ years of denying the molestation, I was very surprised to hear this come from her mouth. I shouted with great joy after hearing her words. I thought that I would never hear my mother ever acknowledge what happened to me. I embraced my mother, kissed her cheeks, cried and thanked her!

After enduring over 11 years of molestation, my mother got into a relationship with my next abuser. When I was 16 years old, I was raped by my mother's then live in boyfriend. He entered my bedroom in the middle of the night, while my mother was at work. I remember him grabbing me, began raping me and I bit him as hard as I could on his chest. Once he was finished, he left my room, like nothing happened. When he went back into their bedroom, I climbed out of my bedroom window, I ran away to a friend's home and called the police. I was removed from my mother's care by the Child Protection Services Agency, and I spent the night in a foster home.

I was removed from the home and placed in the care of my maternal grandmother. I stayed there until I was 17 years old and this is when I married my abusive husband. I suffered from both verbal and physical abuse in front of my (3) three children, at his hands for 10 years before I found the courage to finally leave; but only after being hospitalized for an extended period.

There was not a day that I didn't endure some form of abuse from him. He moved me around away from my family. He wouldn't let me answer the house phone nor could I check the mail. I attempted my first suicide when I was 19 years of age with 2 children. He never visited me in the hospital, nor did he attend any therapy sessions with me. I would attempt suicide 3 more times before the marriage was over. I didn't realize that I was being controlled and abused until I encountered another woman who had gone through what I was currently experiencing.

I thank GOD every single day for this woman, because she opened my eyes to what I was not seeing. She helped me to find the courage to leave my abuser and I did. I did it without looking back and I have not been abused since.

My ex-husband told me that I was worthless, uneducated and that no one would ever want me nor would anyone love me. And the sad thing is, I BELIEVED HIM. I allowed this man to control my thoughts, my feelings and my life. Wow looking back over this part of my life, I can now say I have grown from it, learned from it and can actually say that I will never ever allow another human being to treat me that way again. I have had enough with it all and was determined to STOP the cycle of violence with me.

I can honestly say that experiencing child molestation and the horrific act of rape, I began to have all types of issues and can honestly say that these issues resurfaced in my adult life; with trusting men, sexual intercourse and communication problems. I found myself in years of counseling; whereas, I spoke my truth and my feelings to an empty chair which my counselor said represented my mother. Because my mother was the root of all my anxiety issues and my lack of trust and believing in myself, because my mother failed me. My mother didn't teach me how to be a woman, she didn't teach me how to be a mother, nor did she teach me how to love unconditionally. I had to forgive my mother for her choosing her mates over me, not one, but twice for me to heal.

Since leaving my abusive marriage, I have accomplished goals that I never thought I would or at least what he convinced me of. I have graduated from college three (3) times. I have an Associates of Science in Criminal Justice, Bachelor of Science in Criminal Justice, with a minor in Juvenile Delinquency, a Post Bachelorette Certificate in Not-For-Profit Management and a dual Master's Degree in Public Management and Criminal Justice. I continue to educate myself so that I can instill in others what that one lady instilled in me.

I started a not-for-profit agency that conducted and sponsored conferences and seminars against child abuse, child molestation, rape and domestic violence. I still have the scrap book of all the newspaper articles of the actual programs that I sponsored. I wonder how he would feel if he could read them. I have and continue to be a motivational speaker and activist against violence against women and children.

If they are afraid to speak, I will speak for them. For I am no longer afraid, and he no longer stands upon my vocal cords causing me to be voiceless. I wrote the song "Look at Me Now" because it makes me think of the things, he said to me on a regular basis. In the end I have the last laugh because GOD had and continues to have control and predetermination of my life. Without my faith and the belief that I have in GOD, I would have caved in and my not be here to write my testimony to share with other women in this world.

Believe me when I say that you can walk away and walk away in perfect health. If you are experience any form of violence, PLEASE GET OUT BEFORE IT IS TOO LATE! YOU ONLY HAVE ONE LIFE AND YOU ARE PREDESTINED BY GOD FOR YOUR WORTH!

Don't live through your own life's experiences because they may kill you. Please learn by mine and walk away and live your life to the fullest possible.

Look At Me Now
(Author: Tawana D. Pruitt)

Look at me now
To bad you let me walk out the door
Look at me now
What we had can't be no more
Because you are a day late
And a dollar short
Look at me now

You said I wouldn't make it
That I was no good
That no one would ever want me
Or ever even love me

You said I was ugly
And even skinny too
That I was dummy
Too scared to leave you

Look at me now
To bad you let me walk out the door
Look at me now
What we had can't be no more
Because you are a day late
And a dollar short
Look at me now

Valuable Information

At least 42% of women and 20% of men sustain minor injuries such as scratches, bruises and swelling. More severe injuries may occur if the abuse is frequent and harsh. Pelvic pain, headaches, back pain, broken bones, gynecological injuries, pregnancy complications, STD's, heart or circulatory injuries are a few injuries that may occur during an abusive relationship, just to name a few.

There are psychological effects of domestic violence as well that may occur. Where there is physical violence there is also emotional abuse. Whether the abuse is physical, verbal or emotional it can have severe psychological consequences for the victim; like depression, loss of hope in the future, suicidal behavior, anxiety, low self-esteem and flashbacks.

The victims of domestic violence are also affected socially. The negative social effects can be the very thing that restricts the victims' ability to escape domestic violence. The abuser manages to: control the access of services that are meant to help the victim; the victim will have strained relationships with authority figures such as health care providers and employees; and the victim may experience isolation from family members, friends and other supportive individuals.

By isolating the victim, the abuser manages to continue to have full control of the victims' thoughts, actions and decisions. The abuser uses this form to continue to have full control of the victim, by instilling his or her thoughts into the victim. Like always telling the victim things like you are ugly, no one will ever want you, you don't deserve to live, you are stupid, and no one loves you.

Rape Statistics

44% of victims are under the age 18.

80% of victims are under the age 30.

Every 2 minutes, someone in the U.S. is sexually assaulted.

Each year, there are about victims of sexual assault 207,754.

54% of sexual assaults are not reported to police.

97% of rapists will never spend a day in jail.

Approximately 2/3 of assaults are committed by someone known to the victim.

38% of rapists are a friend or acquaintance.

Rapist Types

Power Rapist – Goal to Humiliate
   Power Reassurance (gentleman rapist, opportunity rapist, compensatory)

   Power Assertive (entitlement, exploitative, can be a date rapist)

Anger Retaliatory – Goal to Torture
   Anger Retaliatory (displaced anger)

   Anger Excitation (sadistic)

Child Abuse Statistics

A report of child abuse is made every 10 seconds.

More than five children die every day as a result of child abuse.

Approximately 80% of children that die from abuse are under the age of 4.

It is estimated that between 50 – 60% of child fatalities due to maltreatment are not recorded as such on-death certificates.

More than 90% of juvenile sexual abuse victims know their perpetrator in some way.

Child abuse occurs at every socioeconomic level, across ethnic and cultural lines, within all religions and at all levels of education.

About 30% of abused and neglected children will later abuse their own children, continuing the horrible cycle of abuse.

About 80% of 21-year old that were abused as children met criteria for at least one psychological disorder.

The estimated annual cost of child abuse and neglect in the United States for year 2008 was $124 billion.

Child Abuse and Criminal Behavior

14% of all men in prison in the USA were abused as children.

36% of all women in prison were abused as children.

Children who experience child abuse & neglect are 59% more likely to be arrested as a juvenile, 28% more likely to be arrested as an adult, and 30% more likely to commit violent crime.

Child Abuse and Substance Abuse

One-third to two-thirds of child maltreatment cases involve substance use to some degree.

Children whose parents' abuse alcohol and other drugs are three times more likely to be abused and more than four times more likely to be neglected than children from non-abusing families.

As many as two-thirds of the people in treatment for drug abuse reported being abused or neglected as children.

Child Abuse Consequences

Abused children are 25% more likely to experience teen pregnancy.

Abused teens are less likely to practice safe sex, putting them at greater risk for STDs

Types of Child Abuse

Neglect - 78.3%
Physical Abuse - 17.6%
Sexual Abuse - 9.2%
Psychological/Maltreatment - 8.1%
Medical Neglect - 2.4%
Other - 10.3%

These percentages sum to more than 100% because a child may have suffered more than one type of maltreatment.

Hotline Numbers

Rape, Abuse, Incest, National Network (RAINN)
1.800.656.HOPE (1-800-656-4673)
National Sexual Assault Hotline

Child Abuse - 1.800.4.A.CHILD
(800 422 4453)
National Child Abuse Hotline

Domestic Violence - 1.800.799.SAFE
National Domestic Violence Hotline

Adolescent Suicide Hotline
800-621-4000

Adolescent Crisis Intervention & Counseling Nineline
1-800-999-9999

AIDS National Hotline
1-800-342-2437

CHADD-Children & Adults with Attention Deficit/Hyperactivity Disorder
1-800-233-4050

Cocaine Help Line
1-800-COCAINE
(1-800-262-2463)

Domestic Violence Hotline
800-799-7233

Drug & Alcohol Treatment Hotline
800-662-HELP

Ecstasy Addiction
1-800-468-6933

Eating Disorders Center
1-888-236-1188

Family Violence Prevention Center
1-800-313-1310

Gay & Lesbian National Hotline
1-888-THE-GLNH (1-888-843-4564)

Suicide Prevention
1-800-850-8078

Healing Woman Foundation (Abuse)
1-800-477-4111

Help Finding a Therapist
1-800-THERAPIST (1-800-843-7274)

Incest Awareness Foundation
1-888 -547-3222

Learning Disabilities
1-888-575-7373

(National Center For)
Missing & Exploited Children
Hotline
1-800-843-5678

National Alliance on Mental
Illness (NAMI)
1-800-950-NAMI (6264)

Panic Disorder Information Hotline
800- 64-PANIC

Post Abortion Trauma
1-800-593-2273

Project Inform HIV/AIDS Treatment
Hotline
800-822-7422

Rape (People Against Rape)
1-800-877-7252

Runaway Hotline - 800-621-4000

Self-Injury (Information only)
(NOT a crisis line. Info and
referrals only)
1-800-DONT CUT (1-800-366-8288)

Sexual Assault Hotline
1-800-656-4673

Sexual Abuse - Stop It Now!
1-888-PREVENT

STD Hotline - 1-800-227-8922

Suicide Prevention Lifeline
1-800-273-TALK

Suicide & Crisis Hotline
1-800-999-9999

Suicide Prevention - The Trevor Helpline
(Specializing in gay and lesbian youth suicide prevention).
1-800-850-8078
Teen Helpline - 1-800-400-0900

Victim Center
1-800-FYI-CALL (1-800-394-2255)

Youth Crisis Hotline
800-HIT-HOME

Exit

Psalm 23:1 KJV reads, the LORD is my shepherd, I shall not want. I believe that the entire 23 Psalm should be a driving force for all women, whether they are being abused or not!

The cycle of violence is a known trend that women tend to find themselves in. Some may be exposed to domestic violence while growing up as a child. When they become women, they look for men who remind them of their fathers.

Some are blessed to have the fortunate opportunity to know that if a man is abusive, that he is not the man for you. Some find themselves stuck and seem to not be able to find a way out of it. If you find that you are in the situation, I say to you to do. YOU CAN GET OUT OF THIS! YOU ARE BETTER THAN HE SAYS YOU ARE! YOU ARE SOMEBODY THAT DESERVES BETTER! THAT YOU ARE GOD'S CHILD! WALK AWAY, STAY ALIVE AND PRAISE GOD FOR THE BLOOD THAT HE SHED FOR YOU! LOOK AT YOURSELF AND SAY "LORD, HELP ME. I NEED YOU TO STEP IN AND GIVE ME THE STRENGTH TO LEAVE AND TO STAY AWAY!

The women in this book were fortunate to know that their

strength was in GOD and the faith that was within them helped to release them from these less fortunate situations.

It is not okay to hit another person. It is not okay to verbally abuse another person. Always remember that it is not okay, that it is wrong, and it is against the law.

Made in the USA
Columbia, SC
16 June 2019